'Can I bear
to leave these
blue hills?'

WANG WEI
Born c.699
Died c.761

LI PO
Born 701
Died 762

TU FU
Born 712
Died 770

WANG IN PENGUIN CLASSICS
Poems

LI AND TU IN PENGUIN CLASSICS
Poems

THREE TANG DYNASTY POETS

Translated by
G. W. Robinson and Arthur Cooper

PENGUIN BOOKS

PENGUIN CLASSICS

UK | USA | Canada | Ireland | Australia
India | New Zealand | South Africa

Penguin Books is part of the Penguin Random House group of companies
whose addresses can be found at global.penguinrandomhouse.com.

Penguin
Random House
UK

This selection published in Penguin Classics 2015
003

Set in 9/12.4 pt Baskerville 10 Pro
Typeset by Jouve (UK), Milton Keynes
Printed in Great Britain by Clays Ltd, St Ives plc

A CIP catalogue record for this book is available from the British Library

ISBN: 978–0–141–39820–4

www.greenpenguin.co.uk

MIX
Paper from
responsible sources
FSC® C018179

Penguin Random House is committed to a
sustainable future for our business, our readers
and our planet. This book is made from Forest
Stewardship Council® certified paper.

Contents

WANG WEI (WANG YOUCHENG)

LI PO (LI BAI)

TU FU (DU FU)

WANG WEI
(WANG YOUCHENG)

Song of the Peach Tree Spring

A fisherman sailed up a river
                    he loved spring in the hills

On both banks peach blossom
                    closed over the farther reaches

He sat and looked at the red trees
                    not knowing how far he was

And he neared the head of the green stream
                    seeing no one

A gap in the hills, a way through
                    twists and turns at first

Then hills gave on to a vastness
                    of level land all round

From far away all seemed
                    trees up to the clouds

He approached, and there were many houses
                    among flowers and bamboos

Foresters meeting would exchange
                    names from Han times

And the people had not altered
                    the Ch'in style of their clothes

They had all lived near
                    the head of Wuling River

And now cultivated their rice and gardens
                                    out of the world

Bright moon and under the pines
                                    outside their windows peace

Sun up and among the clouds
                                    fowls and dogs call

Amazed to hear of the world's intruder
                                    all vied to see him

And take him home and ask him
                                    about his country and place

At first light in the alleys
                                    they swept the flowers from their
                                        gates

At dusk fishermen and woodmen
                                    came in on the stream

They had first come here
                                    for refuge from the world

And then had become immortals
                                    and never returned.

Who, clasped there in the hills,
                                    would know of the world of men?

And whoever might gaze from the world
                                    would make out only clouds and
                                        hills

The fisherman did not suspect
                 that paradise is hard to find

And his earthy spirit lived on
                 and he thought of his own
                 country

So he left that seclusion not reckoning
                 the barriers of mountain and
                 stream

To take leave at home and then return
                 for as long as it might please him.

He was sure of his way there
                 could never go wrong

How should he know that peaks and valleys
                 can so soon change?

When the time came he simply remembered
                 having gone deep into the hills

But how many green streams
                 lead into cloud-high woods –

When spring comes, everywhere
                 there are peach blossom streams

No one can tell which may be
                 the spring of paradise.

Marching song

The bugle is blown and rouses the marchers
With a great hubbub the marchers rise
The wailing notes set the horses neighing
As they struggle across the Golden River
The sun dropping down on the desert's rim
Martial sounds among smoke and dust
We will get the rope round that great king's neck
Then home to do homage to our Emperor.

The Green Stream

To get to the Yellow Flower River
I always follow the green water stream
Among the hills there must be a thousand twists
The distance there cannot be fifty miles
There is the murmur of water among rocks
And the quietness of colours deep in pines
Lightly lightly drifting water-chestnuts
Clearly clearly mirrored reeds and rushes
I have always been a lover of tranquillity
And when I see this clear stream so calm
I want to stay on some great rock
And fish for ever on and on.

The distant evening view when the weather has cleared

The sky has cleared and there is the vast plain
And so far as the eye can see no dust in the air
There is the outer gate facing the ford
And the village trees going down to the mouth of the
    stream
The white water shining beyond the fields
The blue peaks jutting behind the hills
This is no time for leisure on the land –
All hands at work in the fields to the south.

On leaving the Wang River retreat

At last I put my carriage in motion
Go sadly out from the ivied pines
Can I bear to leave these blue hills?
And the green stream – what of that?

A walk on a winter day

I walk out of the city by the eastern gate
And try to send my gaze a thousand miles
Blue hills crossed with green woods
Red sun round on the level plain
North of the Wei you get to Hantan
East of the Pass you go out to Han valley
This was where the Ch'in demesnes met
This was where the governors came to court
The cocks called in Hsienyang
And officers of state struggled for precedence
Ministers called on noblemen
Dukes assembled for official banquets
But Hsiang-ju became old and ill
And had to retire alone to Wuling.

*Passing the mountain cloister of the holy man,
T' an-hsing, at Kanhua Temple*

In the evening he took his fine cane
And paused with his guests at the head of Tiger Stream
Urged us to listen for the sound in the mountains
Then went along by the water back to his house
    Profusion of lovely flowers in the wilds
    Vague sound of birds in the valley
When he sits down tonight the empty hills will be still
And the pine wind will suggest autumn.

Return to Mount Sung

The river ran clear between luxuriant banks
And my carriage jogged along on its way
And the water seemed to flow with a purpose
And in the evening the birds went back together –
Desolate town confronting an old ford
Setting sun filling the autumn hills
After a long journey, at the foot of Mount Sung
I have come home and shut my door.

Seeing off Ch'en Tzu-fu to the east of the Yangtze

Under the willows at the ford
                 there are few travellers left

As the boatman steers away
                 to the other curving shore

But my thoughts will follow you
                 like the spring's returning colours

Returning from south of the Yangtze
                 back to the north.

Song of the Kansu frontier

Two miles galloping all the way
Another one plying the whip –
A message arrives from headquarters
The Huns have surrounded Chouch'üan
The frontier passes are all flying snow
Beacons are out, no smoke.

Good-bye to Li, Prefect of Tzŭchou

In endless valleys trees reaching to the sky
In numberless hills the call of cuckoos
And in those hills half is all rain
Streaming off branches to multiply the springs –
The native women will bring in local cloth
The men will bring you actions about potato fields
Your revered predecessor reformed their ways
And will you be so bold as to repudiate him?

Watching a farewell

Green green the willowed road
The road where they are separating
A loved son off for far provinces
Old parents left at home

He must go or they could not live
But his going revives their grief
A charge to his brothers – gently
A word to the neighbours – softly
A last drink at the gates
And then he takes leave of his friends

Tears dried, he must catch up his companions
Swallowing grief, he sets his carriage in motion
At last the carriage passes out of sight
But still at times there's the dust thrown up from the road

I too, long ago, said good-bye to my family
And when I see this, my handkerchief is wet with tears.

My Chungnan retreat

Middle-aged, much drawn to the Way
Settled for my evening in the Chungnan foothills
Elation comes and off I go by myself
Where are the sights that I must know alone
I walk right on to the head of a stream
I sit and watch when clouds come up
Or I may meet an old woodman –
Talk, laughter, never a time to go home.

Taking the cool of the evening

Thousands of trunks of huge trees
Along the thread of a clear stream
Ahead the great estuary over which
Comes the far wind unobstructed
Rippling water wets white sands
Silver sturgeon swim in transparency
I lie down on a wet rock and let
Waves wash over my slight body
I rinse my mouth and wash my feet
Opposite there's an old man fishing.
How many fish come to the bait –
East of the lotus leaves – useless to think about it.

LI PO (LI BAI)

Drinking with a Gentleman of Leisure in the Mountains

We both have drunk their birth,
    the mountain flowers,
A toast, a toast, a toast,
    again another:

I am drunk, long to sleep;
    Sir, go a little –
Bring your lute (if you like)
    early tomorrow!

In the Mountains: A Reply to the Vulgar

They ask me where's the sense
    on jasper mountains?
I laugh and don't reply,
    in heart's own quiet:

Peach petals float their streams
    away in secret
To other skies and earths
    than those of mortals.

Marble Stairs Grievance

On Marble Stairs
still grows the white dew
　That has all night
soaked her silk slippers,

　But she lets down
her crystal blind now
　And sees through glaze
the moon of autumn.

Letter to His Two Small Children Staying in Eastern Lu at Wen Yang Village under Turtle Mountain

Here in Wu Land mulberry leaves are green,
Silkworms in Wu have now had three sleeps:

My family, left in Eastern Lu,
Oh, to sow now Turtle-shaded fields,
Do the spring things I can never join,
Sailing Yangtze always on my own –

Let the South Wind blow you back my heart,
Fly and land it in the Tavern court
Where, to the East, there are sprays and leaves
Of one peach-tree, sweeping the blue mist;

This is the tree I myself put in
When I left you, nearly three years past;
A peach-tree now, level with the eaves,
And I sailing cannot yet turn home!

Pretty daughter, P'ing-yang is your name,
Breaking blossom, there beside my tree,
Breaking blossom, you cannot see me
And your tears flow like the running stream;

And little son, Po-ch'in you are called,
Your big sister's shoulder you must reach
When you come there underneath my peach,
Oh, to pat and pet you too, my child!

I dreamt like this till my wits went wild,
By such yearning daily burned within;
So tore some silk, wrote this distant pang
From me to you living at Wen Yang . . .

Remembering the East Ranges

1

Long since I turned
to my East Ranges:
    How many times
have their roses bloomed?

    Have their white clouds
risen and vanished
    And their bright moon
set among strangers?

2

But I shall now
take Duke Hsieh's dancers:
    With a sad song
we shall leave the crowds

    And call on him
in the East Ranges,
    Undo the gate,
sweep back the white clouds!

For His Wife

Three-sixty days with a muddled sot,
   That is Mistress Li Po's lot:
In what way different from the life
   Of the Grand Permanent's wife?

The Ballad of Ch'ang-Kan

(The Sailor's Wife)

1

I with my hair fringed on my forehead,
Breaking blossom, was romping outside:

And you rode up on your bamboo steed,
Round garden beds we juggled green plums;
Living alike in Ch'ang-kan village
We were both small, without doubts or guile . . .

When at fourteen I became your bride
I was bashful and could only hide
My face and frown against a dark wall:
A thousand calls, not once did I turn;

I was fifteen before I could smile,
Long to be one, like dust with ashes:
You'd ever stand by pillar faithful,
I'd never climb the Watcher's Mountain!

I am sixteen but you went away
Through Ch'ü-t'ang Gorge, passing Yen-yü Rock
And when in June it should not be passed,
Where the gibbons cried high above you.

Here by the door our farewell footprints,
They one by one are growing green moss,
The moss so thick I cannot sweep it,
And fallen leaves: autumn winds came soon!

September now: yellow butterflies
Flying in pairs in the west garden;
And what I feel hurts me in my heart,
Sadness to make a pretty face old . . .

Late or early coming from San-pa,
Before you come, write me a letter:
To welcome you, don't talk of distance,
I'll go as far as the Long Wind Sands!

2

I remember, in my maiden days
I did not know the world and its ways;
Until I wed a man of Ch'ang-kan:
Now, on the sands, I wait for the winds . . .

And when in June the south winds are fair,
I think: Pa-ling, it's soon you'll be there;
September now, and west winds risen,
I wish you'll leave the Yangtze Haven;

But, go or come, it's ever sorrow
For when we meet, you part tomorrow:
You'll make Hsiang-tan in how many days?
I dreamt I crossed the winds and the waves

Only last night, when the wind went mad
And tore down trees on the waterside
And waters raced where the dark wind ran
(Oh, where was then my travelling man?)

That we both rode dappled cloudy steeds
Eastward to bliss in Isles of Orchids:
A drake and duck among the green reeds,
Just as you've seen on a painted screen . . .

Pity me now, when I was fifteen
My face was pink as a peach's skin:
Why did I wed a travelling man?
Waters my grief . . . my grief in the wind!

The Ballad of Yü-Chang

A Tartar wind blows on Tai horses
Thronging northward through the Lu-yang Gap:

Wu cavalry like snowflakes seaward
Riding westward know of no return,
Where as they ford the Shang-liao shallows
A yellow cloud stares faceless on them;

An old mother parting from her son
Calls on Heaven in the wild grasses,
The white horses round flags and banners,
Sadly she keens and clasps him to her:

'"Poor white poplar in the autumn moon,
Soon it was felled on the Yü-chang Hills" –
You were ever a peaceful scholar,
You were not trained to kill and capture!'

'How can you weep for death in battle,
To free our Prince from stubborn bandits?
Given pure will, stones swallow feathers,
How can you speak of fearing dangers?

'Our towered ships look like flying whales
Where the squalls race on Fallen Star Lake:
This song you sing – if you sing loudly,
Three armies' hair will streak, too, with grey!'

Hard is the Journey

Gold vessels of fine wines,
    thousands a gallon,
Jade dishes of rare meats,
    costing more thousands,

I lay my chopsticks down,
    no more can banquet,
And draw my sword and stare
    wildly about me:

Ice bars my way to cross
    the Yellow River,
Snows from dark skies to climb
    the T'ai-hang Mountains!

At peace I drop a hook
    into a brooklet,
At once I'm in a boat
    but sailing sunward . . .

    (Hard is the Journey,
    Hard is the Journey,
    So many turnings,
    And now where am I?)

So when a breeze breaks waves,
    bringing fair weather,
I set a cloud for sails,
    cross the blue oceans!

Old Poem

Did Chuang Chou dream
he was the butterfly,
   Or the butterfly
that it was Chuang Chou?

In one body's
metamorphoses,
   All is present,
infinite virtue!

You surely know
Fairyland's oceans
   Were made again
a limpid brooklet,

Down at Green Gate
the melon gardener
   Once used to be
Marquis of Tung-ling?

Wealth and honour
were always like this:
   You strive and strive,
but what do you seek?

TU FU (DU FU)

Lament by the Riverside

The old man from Shao-ling,
　　weeping inwardly,
Slips out by stealth in spring
　　and walks by Serpentine,

And on its riverside
　　sees the locked Palaces,
Young willows and new reeds
　　all green for nobody;

Where Rainbow Banners once
　　went through South Gardens,
Gardens and all therein
　　with merry faces:

First Lady of the Land,
　　Chao-yang's chatelaine,
Sits always by her Lord
　　at board or carriage,

Carriage before which Maids
　　with bows and arrows
Are mounted on white steeds
　　with golden bridles;

They look up in the air
　　and loose together,
What laughter when a pair
　　of wings drop downward,

What bright eyes and white teeth,
    but now where is she?
The ghosts of those by blood
    defiled are homeless!

Where limpid River Wei's
    waters flow Eastward,
One goes, the other stays
    and has no tidings:

Though Pity, all our hours,
    weeping remembers,
These waters and these flowers
    remain as ever;

But now brown dusk and horse-
    men fill the City,
To gain the City's South
    I shall turn Northward!

From *The Journey North: the Homecoming*

Slowly, slowly we tramped country tracks,
With cottage smoke rarely on their winds:
Of those we met, many suffered wounds
Still oozing blood, and they moaned aloud!

I turned my head back to Feng-hsiang's camp,
Flags still flying in the fading light;
Climbing onward in the cold hills' folds,
Found here and there where cavalry once drank;

Till, far below, plains of Pin-chou sank,
Ching's swift torrent tearing them in two;
And 'Before us the wild tigers stood',
Had rent these rocks every time they roared:

Autumn daisies had begun to nod
Among crushed stones waggons once had passed;
To the great sky then my spirit soared,
That secret things still could give me joy!

Mountain berries, tiny, trifling gems
Growing tangled among scattered nuts,
Were some scarlet, sands of cinnabar,
And others black, as if lacquer-splashed:

By rain and dew all of them were washed
And, sweet or sour, equally were fruits;
They brought to mind Peach-tree River's springs,
And more I sighed for a life misspent!

Then I, downhill, spied Fu-chou far off
And rifts and rocks quickly disappeared
As I ran down to a river's edge,
My poor servant coming far behind;

There we heard owls hoot from mulberry
Saw fieldmice sit upright by their holes;
At deep of night crossed a battlefield,
The chill moonlight shining on white bones

Guarding the Pass once a million *men*,
But how many ever left this Pass?
True to orders half the men in Ch'in
Here had perished and were alien ghosts!

I had fallen, too, in Tartar dust
But can return with my hair like flour,
A year but past, to my simple home
And my own wife, in a hundred rags;

Who sees me, cried like the wind through trees
Weeps like the well sobbing underground
And then my son, pride of all my days,
With his face, too, whiter than the snows

Sees his father, turns his back to weep –
His sooty feet without socks or shoes;
Next by my couch two small daughters stand
In patched dresses scarcely to their knees

And the seawaves do not even meet
Where old bits of broidery are sewn;
Whilst the Serpent and the Purple Bird
On the short skirts both are upside-down

'Though your father is not yet himself,
Suffers sickness and must rest some days,
How could his script not contain some stuffs
To give you all, keep you from the cold?

'You'll find there, too, powder, eyebrow black
Wrapped in the quilts, rather neatly packed.'
My wife's thin face once again is fair,
Then the mad girls try to dress their hair:

Aping mother in her every act,
Morning make-up quickly smears their hands
Till in no time they have spread the rouge,
Fiercely painted great, enormous brows!

I am alive, with my children, home!
Seem to forget all that hunger, thirst:
These quick questions, as they tug my beard,
Who'd have the heart now to stop and scold?

Turning my mind to the Rebel Camp,
It's sweet to have all this nonsense, noise . . .

The Visitor

North and South of our hut
    spread the Spring waters,
And only flocks of gulls
    daily visit us;

For guests our path is yet
    unswept of petals,
To you our wattle gate
    the first time opens:

Dishes so far from town
    lack subtle flavours,
And wine is but the rough
    a poor home offers;

If you agree, I'll call
    my ancient neighbour
Across the fence, to come
    help us finish it!

Nine Short Songs: Wandering Breezes: 1

The withies near my door
   are slender, supple
And like the waists of maids
   of fifteen summers:

Who said, when morning came,
   'Nothing to mention'?
A mad wind has been here
   and broke the longest!

Nine Short Songs: Wandering Breezes: 8

The catkins line the lanes,
   making white carpets,
And leaves on lotus streams
   spread like green money:

Pheasants root bamboo shoots,
   nobody looking,
While ducklings on the sands
   sleep by their mothers.

The Ballad of the Ancient Cypress

In front of K'ung-ming Shrine
    stands an old cypress,
With branches like green bronze
    and roots like granite;

Its hoary bark, far round,
    glistens with raindrops,
And blueblack hues, high up,
    blend in with Heaven's:

Long ago Statesman, King
    kept Time's appointment,
But still this standing tree
    has men's devotion;

United with the mists
    of ghostly gorges,
Through which the moon brings cold
    from snowy mountains.

(I recall near my hut
    on Brocade River
Another Shrine is shared
    by King and Statesman

On civil, ancient plains
    with stately cypress:
The paint there now is dim,
    windows shutterless . . .)

Wide, wide though writhing roots
   maintain its station,
Far, far in lonely heights,
   many's the tempest

When its hold is the strength
   of Divine Wisdom
And straightness by the work
   of the Creator . . .

Yet if a crumbling Hall
   needed a rooftree,
Yoked herds would, turning heads,
   balk at this mountain:

By art still unexposed
   all have admired it;
But axe though not refused,
   who could transport it?

How can its bitter core
   deny ants lodging,
All the while scented boughs
   give Phoenix housing?

Oh, ambitious unknowns,
   sigh no more sadly:
Using timber as big
   was never easy!

From a Height

The winds cut, clouds are high,
  apes wail their sorrows,
The ait is fresh, sand white,
  birds fly in circles;

On all sides fallen leaves
  go rustling, rustling,
While ceaseless river waves
  come rippling, rippling:

Autumn's each faded mile
  seems like my journey
To mount, alone and ill,
  to this balcony;

Life's failures and regrets
  frosting my temples,
And wretched that I've had
  to give up drinking.

Ballad on Seeing a Pupil of the Lady Kung-Sun Dance the Sword Mime

On the 19th day of the Tenth Month of Year II of Ta-li (15 November 767), I saw the Lady Li, Twelfth, of Lin-ying dance the Mime of the Sword at the Residence of Lieutenant-Governor Yüan Ch'i of K'uei Chou Prefecture; and both the subtlety of her interpretation and her virtuosity on points so impressed me that I asked of her, who had been her Teacher? She replied: 'I was a Pupil of the great Lady Kung-sun!'

In Year V of K'ai-yüan (A.D. 717), when I was no more than a tiny boy, I remember being taken in Yü-yen City to see Kung-sun dance both this Mime and 'The Astrakhan Hat'.

For her combination of flowing rhythms with vigorous attack, Kung-sun had stood alone even in an outstanding epoch. No member at all of the *corps de ballet*, of any rank whatever, either of the Sweet Spring-time Garden or of the Pear Garden Schools, could interpret such dances as she could; throughout the reign of His Late Majesty, Saintly in Peace and Godlike in War! But where now is that jadelike face, where are those brocade costumes? And I whiteheaded! And her Pupil here, too, no longer young!

Having learned of this Lady's background, I came to realize that she had, in fact, been reproducing faithfully all the movements, all the little gestures, of her Teacher; and I was so stirred by that memory, that I decided to make a Ballad of the Mime of the Sword.

There was a time when the great calligrapher, Chang Hsü of Wu, famous for his wild running hand, had several opportunities of watching the Lady Kung-sun dance this Sword Mime (as it is danced in Turkestan); and he discovered, to his immense delight, that doing so had resulted in marked improvement in his own calligraphic art! From *that*, know the Lady Kung-sun!

> A Great Dancer there was,
>   the Lady Kung-sun,
> And her 'Mime of the Sword'
>   made the World marvel!
>
> Those, many as the hills,
>   who had watched breathless
> Thought sky and earth themselves
>   moved to her rhythms:
>
> As she flashed, the Nine Suns
>   fell to the Archer;
> She flew, was a Sky God
>   on saddled dragon;
>
> She came on, the pent storm
>   before it thunders;
> And she ceased, the cold light
>   off frozen rivers!

Her red lips and pearl sleeves
    are long since resting,
But a dancer revives
    of late their fragrance:

The Lady of Lin-ying
    in White King city
Did the piece with such grace
    and lively spirit

That I asked! Her reply
    gave the good reason
And we thought of those times
    with deepening sadness:

There had waited at Court
    eight thousand Ladies
(With Kung-sun, from the first,
    chief at the Sword Dance);

And fifty years had passed
    (a palm turned downward)
While the winds, bringing dust,
    darkened the Palace

And they scattered like mist
    those in Pear Garden,
On whose visages still
    its sun shines bleakly!

*

But now trees had clasped hands
    at Golden Granary
And grass played its sad tunes
    on Ch'ü-t'ang's Ramparts,

For the swift pipes had ceased
    playing to tortoiseshell;
The moon rose in the East,
    joy brought great sorrow:

An old man knows no more
    where he is going;
On these wild hills, footsore,
    he will not hurry!

Night Thoughts Afloat

By bent grasses
in a gentle wind
    Under straight mast
I'm alone tonight,

    And the stars hang
above the broad plain
    But moon's afloat
in this Great River:

    Oh, where's my name
among the poets?
    Official rank?
'Retired for ill-health.'

    Drifting, drifting,
what am I more than
    A single gull
between sky and earth?

The Story of the Peach Blossom Spring by T'ao Ch'ien (T'ao Yüan-ming)

During the T'aiyüan period of the Ch'in dynasty there was a man of Wuling who lived by fishing. He went along a stream and forgot how far he had gone. Suddenly he found himself in a forest of peach blossom extending several hundred paces along both banks, unmixed with any other sort of tree. The fragrance was lovely, and fallen petals were everywhere. The fisherman was extremely surprised, and continued onwards in the hope of reaching the limit of this forest. The forest ended at the source of the stream. There he came on a hill, and in the hill a small opening, from which there seemed to come some light. So he abandoned his boat and went through the opening. The passage was at first so narrow that a man could only just pass, but after going some fifty paces or so, he found that it widened out into a broad and bright place. On the level ground there were dignified buildings, as well as good ricefields, fine pools, mulberry trees and bamboos. There were roads and lanes criss-crossing, and the sounds of fowls and dogs could be heard. People were coming and going, busy sowing seed, and the clothes of both the men and the women looked foreign. Both the grey-haired elders and the youngest children had an air of natural happiness.

They were much amazed at the sight of the fisherman, and asked him where he had come from, to which he replied fully. They then took him back to one of their houses, put wine before him, killed a fowl, and gave him a meal. When news of this man became known in the village, they all came along to find out about him. They said of themselves that their ancestors, escaping from the troubles of the Ch'in period, had brought away their wives and children and the other inhabitants of their locality to this isolated place, and that subsequently no one had left there. This had led to their being cut off from those outside. They asked what dynasty there was now, they themselves having no knowledge of the Han dynasty, not to mention those of Wei and Ch'in. The fisherman replied fully and precisely to their questions, and they were all dumbfounded. The others all came and invited the man to their houses, and all gave him food and drink. He stayed for several days before taking his leave and departing. The people had meanwhile told him that there was no object in divulging their existence to others.

When he emerged, he regained his boat and retraced his route, noting it at every turn. When he reached the prefecture, he went to the prefect and told his tale. The prefect thereupon dispatched someone to go with him and find the route he had noted, but they lost their way and could not find it again.

Liu Tzŭ-chi of Nanyang, a man of quality, heard the tale and was eager to go off to the place himself. But before anything had been achieved, he was taken ill and died, and since then no one has looked for the stream.

This story is the inspiration for Wang Wei's poem that opens this book.